NAPLES & MARCO ISLAND
The Delaplaine Long Weekend Guide

TABLES OF CONTENTS

WHY NAPLES & MARCO ISLAND? – 5

GETTING ABOUT – 9

WHERE TO STAY – 13

WHERE TO EAT – 22

WHERE TO SHOP – 39

WHAT TO SEE & DO – 47

BUSCH GARDENS – 57

NIGHTLIFE – 71

SPAS – 77

INDEX – 79

OTHER BOOKS BY THE AUTHOR – 82

LONG WEEKEND SERIES

Like you, when I'm heading into a new place, I have bought travel guides and toiled through them hour after hour trying to extract from the book the "essence" of the city or region I was visiting. Sometimes, sadly, I spent more hours reading the book than I did in the town it purported to tell me about. To judge by the size of some of these books, you'd think I was planning on spending my life there, not just a few days.

By including exhaustive detail in their guidebooks, many writers actually end up obscuring the essence of the city they're writing about rather than revealing it.

If you're going to stay two or more weeks in a place, then by all means do your homework. There are hundreds of guides, both in print and online, to assist you.

But if you've only got 3 or 4 days, your needs really are different.

I would want to know:

= **LODGINGS**. What would be the best hotels or B&Bs or inns to choose from? I would want a choice of 4 or 5 places in different budget categories. (For the kid with a backpack will be on a different budget than someone on an expense account. A retired couple will have different wants and needs than a family of four.)

= **RESTAURANTS**. What would be a good selection of restaurants, again within different budget levels, that would represent the area I'm visiting? Again, whether expensive or cheap, which of the thousands of places to eat will give me a feel for the town?

= **ATTRACTIONS**. Of all the attractions and things to do, which are the most important that will leave me with memories that I've really *seen* the place?

= **SHOPPING?** Something different and out of the way reflective of the area. Not the big chains, whether that chain is Tiffany or the Gap. Something local.

Rather than craft a definitive itinerary for you the way many others have done, I've expanded the listings in each section so that you could get a good range of the offerings available—so you can pick and choose among them to craft your own special Long Weekend.

WHY NAPLES & MARCO ISLAND?

A lot of my friends who live in Miami, harried by the unrelenting pace of South Beach, escape along the Tamiami Trail for the completely foreign world that lies two hours away in the laid-back town of Naples.

Naples offers a thoroughly different "escape" from the rigorous pace of Miami that the Florida Keys do not. You can take your flip-flops to the Keys, and you can take your flip-flops to Naples. The difference is one of tone. You won't find a Gucci store in Key West, however. You won't find a cluster of world-class spas either. And won't find a Ritz-Carlton that's rated among the best in the world.

There's a lot of money in Naples. It's the money of Midwesterners who disdain the Miami lifestyle. This is an unabashedly American city whereas Miami long ago ceased to have much in common with America besides its money-laundered currency. The money in Naples is unostentatiously evident in the low-level lifestyle than in the crass and glitzy environs you find in Miami. Among the many who love Naples, it's a perfect world.

MARCO ISLAND

As the largest and northernmost of the Ten Thousand Islands, Marco Island clings like a barnacle to its fishing roots. Marinas on the north end offer everything from fishing charters and boat rentals to sailing excursions and luncheon cruises. It's about a 2-hour drive from Miami on US 41 (the famed Tamiami Trail) or from Fort Lauderdale on I-75.

Visitor Information:

Greater Naples Marco Everglades Convention & Visitors Bureau
239-252-2384 or 800-688-3600
www.paradisecoast.com

GETTING ABOUT

The airport (Southwest Florida International Airport, to be exact) serving Naples is whopping 42 miles from the city, so unless you plan on barely leaving your lodgings during your trip, you're looking at a car rental whether you like it or not.
If, however, you plan on focusing your visit in the Old Town, you can do quite handsomely simply by renting a bike.

BIG MOMMA'S BICYCLES
850 Seagate Dr., Suite F, Naples: 239-263-0728
www.bigmommasbicycles.com

WHERE TO STAY

I always like to offer a choice for those with different budgets. I make three trips to any given destination so your own weekend will be not only memorable, but within your budget.

BELLASERA RESORT LUXURY HOTEL
221 Ninth Street South, Naples: 844-898-4184
www.bellaseranaples.com
Right in the middle of the Old Town you'll find this 4-diamond luxury hotel. Has studios as well as 3-room suites with fully appointed kitchens.

HAWTHORN SUITES NAPLES
3557 Pine Ridge Rd, Naples, 239-593-1300
www.hawthornnaples.com
Nothing fancy, just basic.

HILTON MARCO ISLAND BEACH RESORT
560 S Collier Blvd, Marco Island, 239-394-5000
www.hiltonmarcoisland.com
AAA 4-diamond resort, located off the south coast of Florida, with nearly 300 luxurious rooms that include balconies with full or partial views of the beach. Amenities include a heated outdoor pool, a variety of water sports, a spa offering a variety of treatments, three restaurants, two tennis courts and a fitness center. A variety of tours available including the 10,000 Islands Guided Waverunner Tour.

HYATT HOUSE NAPLES / 5TH AVENUE
1345 5th Avenue South, Naples, 239-775-1000
https://www.hyatt.com/en-US/hotel/florida/hyatt-house-naples-5th-avenue/napxn
NEIGHBORHOOD: Downtown
Overlooking the Gordon River, this somewhat boring 83-room hotel features modern studios and 1- and 2-bedroom suites. When booking, be sure you get a view of the river and the little marinas laid out below the balconies. Otherwise, you're just in another Hyatt with nothing really to distinguish it. Amenities: Complimentary Wi-Fi, satellite TVs, hot breakfast buffet and furnished balconies. Hotel features: 24/7 Fitness center, laundry facilities, pool, and on-site restaurant. Pet friendly (surcharge). Conveniently located near attractions like the Naples Zoo and Naples Pier. Smoke-free hotel.

THE INN ON FIFTH
699 5th Ave. S., Naples: 239-403-8777
www.innonfifth.com
This smallish property with about 90 rooms is right in the heart of the city on happening Fifth Avenue South.

LEMON TREE INN
250 Ninth St., Naples: 239-262-1414
www.lemontreeinn.com
Nicely landscaped, this place is a bargain and it's close to the action on Fifth Avenue South. It's got an "old Florida" look and feel that really works. (They give you lemonade when you check in, a nice touch.) Only 30 rooms. Nice courtyard garden. 8 bocks from the beach. Continental breakfast is free. Pool.

LA PLAYA
9891 Gulf Shore Dr., Naples: 239-597-3123
www.laplayaresort.com
No other hotel has the same immediate access to the beach than La Playa. It's as good as the Ritz, but not quite as elegant. Much more intimate. Voted 12th best resort in the U.S. by Condé Nast readers. Golf, Spa.

MARCO BEACH OCEAN RESORT
480 S Collier Blvd, Marco Island, 239-393-1400 or 800-715-8517
www.marcoresort.com
AAA 4-diamond resort with 98 one- and two-bedroom suites with fully equipped kitchens, all facing the gulf. Guests enter a beautiful Mediterranean-styled lobby. Amenities include swimming pool and pool bar located on the fifth-floor rooftop, a spa, fitness center, rooftop gardens, casual resort dining and four miles of white sand beach.

MARCO ISLAND MARRIOTT RESORT & SPA
400 S Collier Blvd, Marco Island, 239-394-2511
www.marcoislandmarriott.com
This world-class resort, set on three miles of beautiful beachfront property, features eight restaurants, oversized rooms, a luxurious spa with Balinese-influenced treatments, two private 18-hole golf courses, and premier amenities. Guests can enjoy a variety of water sports, parasailing, shelling cruises

and sightseeing tours. Located just miles from Naples and Fort Myers.

NAPLES BAY RESORT
1500 5th Ave. S., Naples: 239-530-1199
www.naplesbayresort.com
In the Old Town, this place has a lot to recommend it. It's next to the shopping on Fifth Avenue, has 6 tennis courts, cottages, marina, a yacht club, a spa and it's still pretty reasonably priced.

THE NAPLES BEACH HOTEL & GOLF CLUB
851 Gulf Shore Blvd. N., Naples: 239-261-2222
www.naplesbeachhotel.com
Old building, lots of charm. Family-owned. 318 rooms and suites, a spa and fitness center, championship golf course, six Har-Tru tennis courts, beach, variety of water sports and free Beach Klub 4 Kids. Check out the **Sunset Beach Bar** as a place to

end the day watching the sunset over the Gulf while enjoying that much-needed cocktail.

OLDE MARCO ISLAND INN & SUITES
100 Palm St, Marco Island. 239-394-3131 or 877-475-3466
www.oldemarcoinn.com
Historic Inn feature 50-plus modern one- and two-bedroom suites. The original 1880s inn now houses Bistro Soleil, an elegant restaurant that serves fine French cuisine courtesy of Chef Denis Meurgue. Amenities include free HBO, Patio gardens, heated pool, and hot tub.

THE RITZ CARLTON
280 Vanderbilt Beach Rd., Naples: 239-598-3300
www.ritzcarlton.com
Hard to beat this place for the ultimate in luxurious lodgings. The **Sand Bar** is actually my favorite thing about this hotel. It's a little bar down by the beach where you feel like you're a million miles from anywhere. To create that illusion when you're really at the edge of one of the best resorts in the world is pretty amazing, but they manage to do it here.

Another beachside spot that serves food is **Gumbo Limbo** just a few feet away. It's a bit larger, serves tropically inspired food and shares the breathtaking views of the Gulf. Even if you're not staying at the RC, meander around this property to have a look at how the other half live. Stop by one of these two places for a bite or a drink just to experience the feel of the hotel voted 9th best hotel in the U.S. by readers of "Travel & Leisure" in 2011. Also a Forbes 4 star property and 5 Diamond. And if you're into pampering, and can afford it, the three-floor Spa here was voted best in Florida by readers of "Spa" magazine.

WHERE TO EAT

CAPRI FISH HOUSE RESTAURANT
203 Capri Blvd, Naples, 239-389-5555
www.caprifishhouse.com
CUISINE: Seafood
DRINKS: Full Bar
SERVING: Lunch & Dinner
PRICE RANGE: $$
Casual seafood eatery that offers a creative menu of tasty treats like alligator nuggets and Salmon Nadine.

Indoor and outdoor dining. Occasional live music. Great spot to watch the sunset.

CITY SEAFOOD
702 Begonia St, Everglades City, 239-695-4700
http://www.cityseafood1.com/
CUISINE: Seafood/Seafood Market
DRINKS: Beer & Wine
SERVING: 6 a.m. – 6 p.m.
PRICE RANGE: $$
NEIGHBORHOOD: Everglades City
I know this is WAY out of town, but if you're driving from one coast to the other, you might want to detour to have lunch or dinner at this great waterside eatery and seafood market. It's a throwback to those old fish shacks you used to see all over this part of Florida decades ago. (I'm old enough to remember, LOL.) Just a beat-up old wood-planked building that looks like it needs a paint job, but it's right on the water, and it couldn't be better if it tried. Great selection of seafood including crab, frog legs and alligator. Favorites: Buffalo shrimp wrap and Stone Crabs. Outdoor seating. Order and wait for your number to be called over the loud speaker. See what I said, nothing fancy.

DOCK AT CRAYTON COVE
845 12th Ave S, Naples, 239-263-9940
http://www.dockcraytoncove.com/
CUISINE: Seafood/American (Traditional)
DRINKS: Full Bar
SERVING: Lunch, & Dinner
PRICE RANGE: $$

NEIGHBORHOOD: Old Naples
Dockside eatery overlooking a vast water expanse and a marina, so you'll want to sit outside if you can. I love this place when a storm passes by—you see the dark clouds forming in the sky over the ocean or the Everglades. You watch them approach and then get the sound of the rain when it starts. Very nice. Also, a good spot at sunset. Rustic interior. Has a menu of seafood and American fare. Nice raw bar selection. Menu picks: Blackened Mahi Fish Tacos, the excellent Lobster and the Crab Stuffed Grouper. Sunday brunch with a make-your-own Bloody Mary bar. Vegan options

H.B.'S ON THE GULF
Naples Beach Hotel
851 Gulf Shore Blvd. N, Naples, 239-435-4347
www.naplesbeachhotel.com
CUISINE: Seafood
DRINKS: Full Bar
SERVING: Lunch & Dinner

PRICE RANGE: $$$
Seafood, seafood, seafood. Nothing to the décor, but the food's really tasty. Lunch, dinner.

JOE'S DINER
9331 Tamiami Trail N. Suite 14, Naples, 239-254-7929
www.joesdiners.com
CUISINE: American
DRINKS: No Booze
SERVING: Breakfast & Lunch
PRICE RANGE: $
Great spot for breakfast. Surly wait staff actually adds to the "experience."

LATITUDE 26
Hyatt House Naples
1345 5th Ave S, Naples, 239-775-1000
https://www.latitude26restaurant.com/
CUISINE: American/Fusion
DRINKS: Full Bar
SERVING: Lunch, & Dinner
PRICE RANGE: $$
NEIGHBORHOOD: Bonita Springs

Located in the Hyatt Hotel, causal waterfront eatery serving modern American fare with a slight Southern twist (but not much). Pretty standard menu for what it is. Nothing different. Favorites: Crab cakes and Black Grouper. The Half-chicken with Peruvian spices is about the most interesting thing on the menu. Vegetarian friendly

LOCAL
5323 Airport Pulling Rd N, Naples, 239-596-3276
www.thelocalnaples.com
CUISINE: Seafood
DRINKS: Beer & Wine Only
SERVING: Lunch & Dinner
PRICE RANGE: $$
Trendy seafood eatery offering a farm-to-table and sea-to-table menu. Great daily specials (including fresh local clams, shrimp, and fish tacos) and nice wine selection. (The BBQ chicken is really good, too, as is the pecan crumble.)

M WATERFRONT GRILLE
4300 Gulf Shore Blvd N, Naples, 239-263-4421
http://mwaterfrontgrille.com/
CUISINE: American (New)/Seafood
DRINKS: Beer & Wine
SERVING: Lunch, & Dinner, Sunday Brunch
PRICE RANGE: $$$
NEIGHBORHOOD: Park Shore
Upscale waterfront eatery serving New American fare with a seafood focus. Favorites: Yellowfin Tuna and Southern Fried Calamari. Gluten-free options. Bottomless champagne Sunday Brunch. Award-winning wine list featuring over 250 wines.

MANGO'S DOCKSIDE BISTRO
760 N Collier Blvd #109, Marco Island, 239-393-2433
https://www.mangosdocksidebistro.com/
CUISINE: Seafood / Sushi / American
DRINKS: Full Bar
SERVING: Breakfast, Lunch, & Dinner
PRICE RANGE: $$
NEIGHBORHOOD: Smokehouse Bay
Spacious family-friendly spot for breakfast, lunch, dinner & cocktails in ultra-casual setting with light wood paneled walls. Has a seafood focused menu. It's in a modern building with a so-so décor, but if you're looking out at the water and the marinas, you won't mind the uninspiring surroundings. Favorites: Conch Chowder; All American breakfast items are good; Fish tacos and Lobster rolls. Gift shop.

MEL'S DINER
3650 Tamiami Trail N, Naples, 239-643-9898
www.melsdiners.com
CUISINE: Diner
DRINKS: Beer & Wine Only
SERVING: Breakfast, Lunch & Dinner
PRICE RANGE: $
There are several of Mel's diners in this part of Florida, and they are all good.

RIVERWALK AT TIN CITY
1200 5th Ave S, Naples, 239-263-2734
http://www.riverwalktincity.com/
CUISINE: Seafood/Diner
DRINKS: Full Bar
SERVING: Lunch, & Dinner
PRICE RANGE: $$
NEIGHBORHOOD: Old Naples
One of many "nautical-style" seafood eateries in this area with both indoor and outdoor seating on the water where you can watch all the boat traffic going by. (There's a lot of it.) This place has a somewhat better menu than most of these types of places. And the "nautical" look is professional enough to make you think they actually hired someone to do it right, not just throw up an old net over a ceiling beam and that's it. Menu picks: Blue Crab Roll and Lobster Quesadilla. Live music.

SALE E PEPE
480 S Collier Blvd, Marco Island, 239-393-1600
www.sale-e-pepe.com.
CUISINE: Italian
DRINKS: Full bar
SERVING: Breakfast, Lunch, Dinner
PRICE RANGE: $$$$
This classy Tuscan-inspired Italian eatery, located at Marco Beach Ocean Resort, overlooks the beach affording beautiful sunset views. Seasonal menu includes authentic house-made pasta, seafood, and meats. Favorites include Smoked Gnocchi with Duck and the Calamata Olive bread. Excellent service, friendly staff.

SEA SALT
1186 Third Street S, Naples, 239-434-7258
seasaltnaples.com
CUISINE: Seafood
DRINKS: Full Bar
SERVING: Lunch & Dinner
PRICE RANGE: $$$
Famous for its emphasis on locally-sourced ingredients. Big emphasis on fish, but don't overlook the Wagyu rib eye. Great Italian wine list with some bargains.

SHULA'S STEAK HOUSE
Hilton Hotel
5111 Tamiami Trail N, Naples, 239-430-4999
www.shulasnaples.com
CUISINE: American, Steakhouses
DRINKS: Full Bar
SERVING: Dinner
PRICE RANGE: $$$$
They have two porterhouses here (24 oz and 48 oz). I've had them both, and I'm not proud of it, but they WERE good.

SNOOK INN
1215 Bald Eagle Dr, Marco Island, 239-394-3313
https://snookinn.com/
CUISINE: Seafood

DRINKS: Full Bar
SERVING: Lunch, & Dinner
PRICE RANGE: $$
NEIGHBORHOOD: Marco Island
Casual waterfront seafood eatery offering beautiful views of Marco Bay from under thatched tiki huts or patio umbrellas. Great place for a drink during sunset. Favorites: Seafood chowder; Grouper sandwiches and Mahi Mahi. Live Music most nights. Nice wine selection. Gift shop.

STAN'S IDLE HOUR
221 Goodland Dr. West, Goodland, 239-394-3041
www.stansidlehour.net
CUISINE: Seafood
DRINKS: Full bar
SERVING: Lunch, Dinner
PRICE RANGE: $$
Dive-type bar with lots of character. Menu includes fresh seafood, burgers, and sandwiches. Weekends only until November. Live music.

SUNSET GRILLE
900 S Collier Blvd, Marco Island, 239-389-0509
www.sunsetgrilleonmarcoisland.com
CUISINE: Pizza, American
DRINKS: Full bar
SERVING: Lunch, Dinner, Brunch
PRICE RANGE: $$
Beachside sports bar, with indoor or outdoor seating, located on Marco Island's beautiful South Beach. Menu favorites like Peel and Eat Gulf Shrimp and the Fried Shrimp Basket. A favorite spot for brunch.

TRIAD SEAFOOD
401 School Dr W, Everglades, 239-695-0722
www.triadseafoodmarketcafe.com
CUISINE: Seafood
DRINKS: Beer & Wine Only
SERVING: Lunch & Dinner; closes 6 p.m. during the week & 7 p.m. on weekends
PRICE RANGE: $$

A family owned and run eatery known for their "All You Can Eat" stone crabs. They sit right on the Barron River not far from the docks where stone crabs are brought in fresh. A screened-in patio is where you will gorge on stone crabs, eating on picnic tables overlooking the water. If it's not stone crab season (which runs from Oct. 15 to May 15), by all means don't overlook this place. They offer superior conch fritters, Key Lime Pie and other seafood. About 20 or 30 minutes east of Marco Island.

TRULUCK'S SEAFOOD, STEAK, AND CRAB HOUSE
698 4th Ave. S, Naples, 239-530-3131
www.trulucks.com
CUISINE: Seafood, Steakhouses
DRINKS: Full Bar
SERVING: Dinner
PRICE RANGE: $$$
Excellent steakhouse, but they also serve up stone crabs in season that rival anyone else's. Plush décor, just what you expect from an Expense Account Steakhouse.

VERDI'S AMERICAN BISTRO
241 N Collier Blvd, Marco Island, 239-394-5533
www.verdisbistro.com.
CUISINE: American, Seafood, Steakhouse
DRINKS: Beer and Wine only
SERVING: Dinner
PRICE RANGE: $$$
Comfortable bistro with good seafood and meat selection. Menu favorites include Sautéed duck, Duck Pot Stickers, Clam chowder, and Short Ribs.

WHERE TO SHOP

Palm-lined **Fifth Avenue South** and **Third Street South** are where you'll find the more interesting shopping opportunities in Naples. (This is the section called Old Naples or Old Town.)
You'll find sidewalk cafes, galleries, quaint little shops with all kinds of interesting merchandise, gift shops, Clothing boutiques. Parking is a pain in the ass, which is why it always makes sense to stay in one of the little hotels in this area.

THE BEACH HOUSE OF NAPLES
1300 Third St S, Naples, 239-261-1366
Waterside Shops, 5455 Tamiami Trail N, Naples, 239-598-4144
www.beachhousenaples.com
This women's boutique specializes in swimwear, resort wear, and swimming accessories. The shop also

carries sandals, beach bags, hats, and cover ups. Carries lines like Seafolly, La Perla, Trina Turk and L*Space.

C. ORRICO
255 13th Ave S, Naples, 239-435-4565
www.corrico.com
Women's boutique specializing in designer resort and beachwear. The latest Lilly Pulitzer fashions are featured here with her emblematic look emblazed on cellphone covers, dresses, bracelets, handbags.

LOUIS VUITTON
5415 Tamiami Trail N. #13, Naples: 239-254-0456
www.louisvuitton.com
The world-renowned leather goods supplier has a store here.

LOVING FINE JEWELRY
879 3rd St. S., Naples, 239-649-7455
Wonderful store featuring one-of-a-kind special pieces.

MARISSA COLLECTIONS
1167 Third St. S., Naples: 239-263-4333
www.marissacollections.com
Top designer names like Oscar de la Renta, Marc Jacobs, Blugirl, Sachin + Babi, Lanvin. Accessories, handbags, jewelry, beauty products, both men's and women's.

MIROMAR OUTLETS
10801 Corkscrew Re., Estero: 239-948-3766
Between Naples & Fort Myers
www.miromaroutlets.com/
Diesel, DKNY, Dolce & Gabbana, Gap, Nike, Gucci, Guess, Hollister, J Crew, Kenneth Cole, Lacoste, Oshkosh B'Gosh, Polo, Puma, Coach, Dooney and Bourke, the Luggage Center, Pottery Barn, Chefs Outlet, Crate and Barrel, Nautical Landing, Restoration Hardware, Waterford crystal and Williams-Sonoma.

OLD NAPLES SURF SHOP
1311 3rd St S, Naples, 239-262-1877
www.oldnaplessurfshop.com
This is the best surf shop in the area, and has been here since 1983—the go-to shop for surf gear and clothing. The shop also sells and rents surfboards, paddleboards, skimboards, and skateboards. Great place to get souvenirs including their own logo line of T-shirts and rash guards. (The staff here leads paddleboard eco-tours, so you're in good hands when you go out there on the briny.)

PEACE, LOVE & LITTLE DONUTS
3106 Tamiami Trail, N. Naples, 239-213-0188
www.peaceloveandlittledonuts.com

If you love donuts this this shop (located in a gas station) is for you, even if you are in one of the most expensive towns on Florida's West Coast. Very creative variety of donuts. Try their key lime pie donut, or the one called Saigon cinnamon, which is really delicious. This is part of a chain that began in Pittsburgh.

TOMMY BAHAMA
1220 Third St., Naples: 239-643-6889
www.tommybahama.com
I go for the crab bisque and the coconut shrimp whenever I swing into this joint. Oops, sorry—come here for the shopping!

WILLIAM PHELPS CUSTOM JEWELER
4380 Gulf Shore Blvd. N., Naples: 239-434-2233
www.phelpsjewelers.com
He does sand castings of shells found on the beach here and then encrusts them with jewels. Lots of other

original art in here as well. They offer a free cleaning and inspection of your jewelry.

WATERSIDE SHOPS
5415 Tamiami Trail N., Naples: 239-598-1605
www.watersideshops.com/
Some of the finest names in luxury retail and fashionable lifestyle stores are set amid a lush landscape of 30,000 tropical plants and flowering shrubs, a 550-foot-long, hand-laid rock wall punctuated by cascading water, and dramatic lightning features. More than 60 shops and restaurants, as well as Saks Fifth Avenue and Nordstrom. De Beers, Hermes, Gucci, Cartier, Coach, Cache, Brooks Brothers, Ann Taylor, Lacoste, Michael Kors, Papyrus, Ralph Lauren.

WHAT TO SEE & DO

BEACHES
Naples is all about the beach, right? The most crowded tourist destination beach is off the Old Town (Fifth Avenue South, Fifth Street South).
Steer away from this area because it's overcrowded. To the north there are lots of hotels, so this too is not so great. If you go south to 18th Avenue South, this is a good place because it's less crowded, and when you go to the beach, you can walk along the sands and

peer up into the grounds of some of the more extravagant mansions of the really rich. Parking can be a hassle during peak times.

CORKSCREW SWAMP SANCTUARY
375 Sanctuary Rd W, Naples, 239-348-9151
http://corkscrew.audubon.org/
Open daily. Moderate admission fee good for entry over two days.
Enjoy a visit to the wilderness that dates back more than 500 years. This unique 2 ¼ mile boardwalk travels through pine flatwoods, wet prairie, around a marsh, and into a Bald Cypress forest – home to hundreds of wildlife including alligators, otters, white-tailed deer, songbirds, and turtles.

DOLPHIN EXPLORER
951 Bald Eagle Dr, Marco Island, 239-642-6899
www.dolphin-study.com
Fee & Reservations necessary.
A 30-foot catamaran powered by two 225 HP outboards crewed by a USCG Master Captain and Mate. Boat can carry up to 28 passengers. Two drips daily (9 a.m. and 1 p.m., with each trip lasting 3 hours). Great way to observe marine life and ideal trip for photographers. This trip has been recognized by National Geographic.

FINDICTIVE CHARTERS
880 12th Ave S., Naples: 239-774-3314
No Website
Half-day or full-day tours available. The personable captain Michael can tailor the trip to fit your needs. Over 20 years fishing these waters.

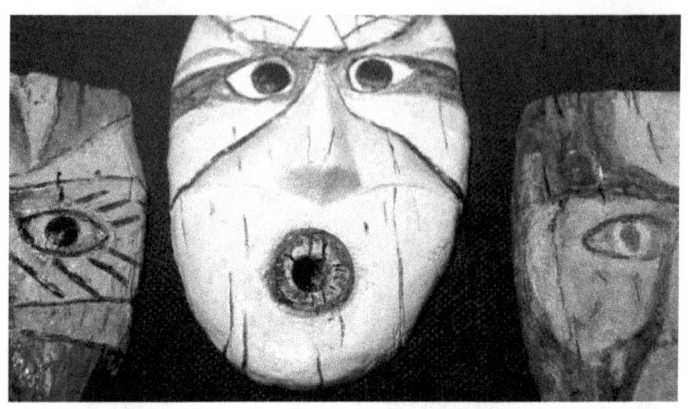

MARCO ISLAND HISTORICAL MUSEUM
180 S Heathwood Dr, Marco Island, 239-642-1440.
https://colliermuseums.com
This museum celebrates Southwest Florida's Calusa Indians and their vanished civilization. Temporary and traveling exhibitions trace the history of the island. Free admission.

NAPLES BOTANICAL GARDEN
4820 Bayshore Dr., Naples: 239-643-7275
naplesgarden.org
It was only as recent as 1993 that 8 residents joined to form this attraction. Their dream was to have a world-class botanical garden, and they have achieved their dream. A financial gift in 2000 from the Katnick family allowed the group to buy a 170-acre plot just south of Old Naples.

The busy Butterfly House is a big attraction, but they have created several themed gardens that will keep you interested: the Asian Garden, the Florida Garden, the Caribbean Garden, the Children's Garden, the Brazilian Garden. Well worth your time.

NAPLES DEPOT MUSEUM
1051 5th Ave S, Naples, 239-252-8419
www.colliermuseums.com
Open Mon – Sat.
Free admission. Located in the restored **Seaboard Air Line Railway** passenger station, this museum takes visitors back to the era of the roaring '20s when traveling by rail was new and in some cases still glamorous. The museum features exhibits of Seminole dugout canoes, a mule wagon, an antique swamp buggy, restored rail cars, and interactive exhibits telling the story of a young Naples and how various transportation modes shaped the city's history. Just behind this museum is the privately-owned **Naples Train Museum** (Open Thurs – Saturday, entry fee) which features an interactive model layout and a train ride for children.
www.naplestrainmuseum.org

NAPLES MUSEUM OF ART
5833 Pelican Bay Blvd., Naples: 239-597-1900
thephil.org
Always has something special they're exhibiting, but it's worth dropping by if you've never seen their permanent collection. It's surprisingly strong on American modernism (big names like Sheeler and Bluemner). Mexican art is represented by names like Orozco and Tamayo. Doesn't ignore local artists, either.

NAPLES ZOO AT CARIBBEAN GARDENS
1590 Goodlette-Frank Rd., Naples: 239-262-5409
www.caribbeangardens.com/
A nationally accredited zoo with animals from alligators to zebras blended into a historic botanical garden. It's basically two attractions in one. Tiger Forest, Panther Glade, and African Oasis. Wildlife presentations all day and a cruise past islands of monkeys.

OTTER MOUND PRESERVE
1831 Addison Ct, Marco Island, 239-252-2961
www.colliergov.net
This 2.45-acre preserve is located in the residential area of Marco Island. The preserve is known for the unique whelk shell terraces of the preserves signature man-made feature. Open all year. Free.

SMALLWOOD STORE
360 Mamie St, Chokoloskee, 239-695-2989
www.smallwoodstore.com

Open daily.
Small museum located on the Chokoloskee Bay.
Formerly a store for the local pioneers, this shop has
now been opened as a museum and serves as a time
capsule of Florida pioneer history. Inside the museum
is the **Tigertail Gift Shop** where you'll find books
and DVDs, authentic Seminole crafts and carvings,
alligator heads, artwork from local artists, t-shirts and
souvenirs.

SUNDAY BASH
STAN'S IDLE HOUR
221 Goodland Dr. West, Goodland, 239-394-3041
www.stansidlehour.net
A weekly celebration featuring dancing women in
feathers and live music. It's also a celebration of the

Buzzard Lope Queen created by Stan. Every Sunday. Closed during summer until Oct. 1.

TENNIS
Arthur L. Allen Tennis Center
Cambier Park (across from City Hall)
735 8TH Ave. S., Naples: 239-213-3060
https://www.naplesgov.com/parksrec/page/arthur-l-allen-tennis-center
Stay away from pricey hotel tennis courts. Come down to these 12 Hydro-Grid (sub-irrigated) lighted Har-Tru (clay-like surface) courts. Meticulously maintained. Open to all. And the rates are cheap, cheap, cheap.

TIGERTAIL BEACH
Marco Island, 239-252-4000
www.tigertailbeach.net
While Marco Island is known for its mega-mansions, resorts and condo towers lining the beach, there's still this pristine, wild and beautiful wide sandy beach in a Collier County park that offers a kid-friendly water area. You may wonder how this beach escaped development. The answer: this used to be a key called Sand Dollar Island. In 2005, Hurricane Wilma deposited hundreds of tons of sand at the southern end of the island, which connected it to the mainland. Instead of walking the long route around to the connecting sandbar, try taking a shortcut by crossing the shallow lagoon. Great place for animal watching and shelling. Kayak rentals available. Nearby café for dining.

TIN CITY
On the river in downtown Naples. Originally a fisherman's wharf (it is still used as such), it is now a large collection of shops (all indoor and air-conditioned) offering a huge array of trinkets, clothing, art, and miscellaneous.

BUSCH GARDENS TAMPA BAY
10165 N McKinley Dr., Tampa, 813-884-4386
www.buschgardens.com
ADMISSION: varies
HOURS: 10 a.m. – 6 p.m.
Busch Gardens Tampa Bay combines world-class thrill rides, Broadway-style live entertainment and one of North America's largest zoos in an unforgettable adventure for the whole family. New in 209, **Iceploration** features world-class skaters, larger-than-life puppets and even animal stars, inspiring audiences to "explore the world" on a journey to the four corners of the earth. Also new, the **Animal Care Center** welcomes guests to closely observe veterinary care and treatment at this new state-of-the-art facility,

a 335-acre 19th century African-themed animal park. It opened on March 31, 1959 as an admission-free hospitality facility for Tampa Anheuser-Busch; in addition to various beer tastings they had, a bird garden and the Stairway to the Stars which was an escalator that took guests to the roof of the brewery.

Busch Gardens continued to grow and in 1965 they opened the 29-acre **Serengeti Plains** which allowed the African wildlife to roam freely. It continued to focus on its tropical landscape, exotic animals, and amusements to draw visitors. Busch Gardens began charging admission as the entertainment became more complex, with extra fees for the thrill rides, such as the roller coasters for which Busch Gardens is now known. Currently Busch Gardens competes with other such parks in Florida and charges comparable fees. The park is operated by SeaWorld Parks & Entertainment, owned by the private equity firm The Blackstone Group. In 2011, the park hosted 4.3 million people, placing in the Top 20 of the most-visited theme parks in the US and in the Top 25 worldwide.

The Serengeti Express (a replica steam train) runs along the back end of the park and makes stops at the Nairobi, Congo and Stanleyville themed areas. The train track was recently renovated, and its tracks have been changed.

The **Skyride** transports guests between Crown Colony and Stanleyville.

MOROCCO
The park's main entrance is home to the Mystic Sheiks of Morocco brass and percussion ensemble.

Treats can be purchased at the Sultan's Sweets and the Zagora Cafe. The Moroccan Palace, a 1,200-seat indoor theatre, is located here, as well as the outdoor Marrakesh Theater. Gwazi is the major ride in this area.

GWAZI, a 105-foot, 50 mph dueling wooden roller coaster named after a mythological creature with the head of a tiger and the body of a lion opened. The dueling sides consist of a lion side and a tiger side, which cross paths seven times. In 2011 Busch Gardens replaced the original trains, which were boxy and sat four per coach. The new trains seat two per coach and should provide a smoother ride. Great Coasters International Inc. designed both the original Gwazi trains and the new Gwazi trains.

Gwazi Gliders, a small hang glider flat ride relocated from the Congo section's defunct Pygmy Village kids' area.

BIRD GARDENS

This is the original section of the park that opened back in 1959. The area for the most part remains to be mostly gardens and animal exhibits/shows. A staple attraction that once stood in this section was the brewery. However, the brewery closed in 1995 and Gwazi now sits where the brewery was located. The traditional, educational bird show is currently being replaced with a newer, more entertainment-based show, including a number of mammals.

WALKABOUT WAY

Themed as an Australian outpost, Walkabout Way opened in June of 2010. This area gives guests the chance to see and hand-feed kangaroos and wallabies. This area is home to a kookaburra, magpie geese and

Australian black swans. This experience is open to all guests 5 years of age or older.

SESAME STREET SAFARI OF FUN

Former Land of the Dragons children's section of the park. Land of the Dragons was replaced by Sesame Street Safari of Fun on March 27, 2010. It contains all the attractions from Land of the Dragons which are now re-themed. It also contains four new attractions: Telly's Jungle Jam, an interactive play area; Rosita's Djembe Fly-Away, a swing ride; Bert & Ernie's Watering hole, a water play area, and Air Grover, a children's roller coaster.

STANLEYVILLE

This section of the park is home to the park's water rides and SheiKra, which was the first and only Dive Coaster in the United States until the addition of Griffon at the sister park Busch Gardens Williamsburg. The section opened up in 1973 with the addition of the Stanley Falls Flume. The African Queen Boat Ride opened in 1977 as Busch's version of Disney's Jungle Cruise. In 1989, the African Queen Boat Ride was transformed into Tanganyika Tidal Wave with the addition of a 55-foot drop that generates a giant splash. The section remained unchanged from then until 2005, when SheiKra opened, and the surrounding area was renovated.

SHEIKRA

a 200-foot Bolliger & Mabillard floorless dive roller coaster with a 90-degree vertical drop. This is Florida's first Floorless Vertical Dive Coaster.

Stanley Falls Flume, a log flume with a 43-foot drop.

Tanganyika Tidal Wave, a 20 passenger shoot the chutes water ride with a 55-foot drop.

CONGO

Python, the park's first roller coaster. It was also Florida's first inverting roller coaster. It was removed in 2006.

This section contains two of the park's more popular rides. In November 2006, Congo underwent major renovation, including the removal of the park's classic Python roller coaster.

KUMBA, meaning roar in Swahili, is a 143-foot steel sit-down roller coaster with seven inversions. Built in 1993 by Bolliger & Mabillard, it still remains a popular ride today.

Congo River Rapids, a water ride that simulates raging whitewater rapids. The ride opened in 1982.

Ubanga Banga Bumper Cars, a bumper cars ride.

JUNGALA

Jungala is a 4-acre family attraction featuring up-close animal encounters, rope bridges to explore three stories of jungle life, and a water-play area for children. Also located in this area are two family attractions: **Jungle Flyers, a zip line** that offers three different flight patterns above the treetops of the new area, and Wild Surge, a shot tower that launches guests above a waterfall. Another attraction is Tiger Trail, which is a walkthrough with tigers where there is also a glass turret where you can look out right in the middle of the tiger enclosure. Stiltwalkers perform and interact with guests in the heart of Jungala during several parts of the day.

Jungle Fliers, a zip line ride.

The Wild Surge, a Moser family launch tower ride.

Python, an Arrow Dynamics looping coaster patterned after the original Corkscrew at Knott's Berry Farm, previously occupied the site occupied now by Jungala.

TIMBUKTU

A section themed after the malls and bazaars of Africa. The Phoenix was built in 1984 and remains a popular ride to this day. The section was renovated in 2003. Important rides added during this facelift included the Timbuktu Theater, which replaced the park's Dolphin Theater with an indoor 4-D movie theater. In 2004, Das Festhaus was transformed into the Desert Grill, and the park's family-friendly Sand Serpent wild mouse roller coaster opened, replacing the Crazy Camel flat ride.

Scorpion, a steel Schwarzkopf-designed sit-down roller coaster with one vertical loop.

Sand Serpent, a steel wild mouse roller coaster.

Phoenix, an Intamin Looping Starship themed as an Egyptian cargo vessel.

Sesame Street Film Festival 4-D a 3-D short film starring characters from Sesame Street. The film is shown in the Timbuktu Theater jointly with Pirates 4-D.

Pirates 4-D a 3-D short film about Pirates starring Leslie Nielsen. It is shown in the Timbuktu Theater jointly with Sesame Street.

Sandstorm, an orbiter ride with six arms that spins riders around. Sandstorm will be relocated to the plaza in front of the Gwazi twin coasters.

Caravan Carousel, a carousel with horses, camels, and chariots.

NAIROBI

Alligators and crocodiles can be observed here up close. In Curiosity Cavern, guests can view mammal and reptile exhibits. Visitors to Nairobi can view injured or abandoned newborns at the Nairobi Field Station Animal Nursery. The area also contains Myombe Reserve, a tropical rainforest that is home to Western Lowland Gorillas and Common Chimpanzees. The major ride here is Rhino Rally, an unpredictable off-road safari that once sent its riders down a raging river. The river portion of the attraction was eventually abandoned due to repeated vehicle breakdowns. In 2012 the Animal Care Center opened. The main train station at Busch Gardens is located at Nairobi. Another popular attraction here is the Asian Elephant exhibit, which is also featured in the Rhino Rally ride.

Rhino Rally, a Vekoma River Adventure ride, Riders board inside modified Land Rovers through the park's Serengeti Plain habitat, interacting with animals.

Animal Care Center, this nearly 16,000 square-foot attraction allows visitors the chance to view the Busch Gardens' veterinarians at work in a new state of the art veterinary hospital. The major visitor aspects of the facility include a nutrition demonstration kitchen, treatment rooms, a clinical lab and an interactive diagnostic activity. Behind the scenes the veterinary hospital also includes the animal nutrition center, animal recovery and holding rooms and vet offices. The park's former animal care center was located behind the scenes.

CROWN COLONY PLAZA
CROWN COLONY HOUSE

Crown Colony is the smallest section of the park. It features a restaurant, the Cheetah Hunt roller coaster, and the Skyride station. 2009 marked the 50th anniversary of Busch Gardens, so a museum was set up, featuring a timeline of pictures, costumes from previous shows, and old maps of the park. It also has a preserved Python roller coaster seat. The museum is still there today.

Cheetah Hunt A multi-launch steel roller coaster that opened in 2011.

Cheetah Run an animal exhibit located next to Cheetah Hunt. It replaced the Clydesdale Hamlet.

EGYPT
Bedouin tents and authentic handicrafts and art

create an Egyptian marketplace feel. Guests can visit a replica of King Tutankhamen's tomb with the excavation in progress. The primary attraction of the Egypt themed area is Montu, an inverted steel coaster.

Montu, named after the Egyptian Falcon God of War, is a 150-foot steel inverted Bolliger & Mabillard roller coaster with seven inversions.

ANIMAL EXHIBITS

CHEETAH RUN

In May 2011, Cheetah Run opened. Cheetah Run is home to Busch Gardens Tampa Bay collection of Cheetahs. There are running demonstrations and meet a keeper throughout the day. In addition, the exhibit has interactive screens with cheetah facts.

The Serengeti Plain

In 1965, the park opened its Serengeti Plain animal habitat, the first of its kind to offer animals in a free-roaming environment. Over the years, the habitat has expanded from 29-acre to its current size of 65-acre. It is home to the Grevy's zebra, reticulated giraffe, bongo, addax, White Rhinoceros, eland, impala, ostrich, marabou stork, East African crowned crane and sacred ibis.

MYOMBE RESERVE
Giraffes at the "Edge of Africa" attraction.
A 3-acre home for six lowland gorillas and nine chimpanzees located in Nairobi, opened in 1992.

EDGE OF AFRICA
Opened in 1997, Edge of Africa is a walk-through attraction where guests can observe African animals. Among the exhibits are a Nile Crocodile, meerkats, two prides of lions, a pack of Spotted Hyenas, two hippos, vultures and a troop of lemurs.

CURIOSITY CAVERNS
This cavern attraction, formerly known as Nocturnal Mountain, contains animals such as bats, snakes, lizards, tamarins, and sugar gliders in the low-light environment. This attraction offers the true facts about the creatures inside and cracks the myths about them wide open.

REAL MUSIC SERIES
From January - March, Busch Gardens hosts a weekly concert series, which invites popular bands either in Big Bands or Pop to perform classic or contemporary songs.
Bands, Brew & BBQ
(Previously called Bud & BBQ) For the month of

February, Busch Gardens hosts a series of concerts in Gwazi Field, from many classic and contemporary Country music acts; there are special culinary offerings along the walkway from the Gwazi Roller Coaster to the gate in Gwazi Field.

Viva La Musica!

In March, several Latin music acts, such as Guyacon, are hosted on the Stage in Gwazi Field. There is a similar culinary setup with special offerings for the concert days as there is for Bands, Brew & BBQ.

Summer Nights

NIGHTLIFE

Now, let's face it—people don't throng to this area of Florida for its pulsating nightlife. But there are a few things to do after the sun descends more gloriously into the Gulf waters here than most places on earth. Herewith, some suggestions:

BLUE MARTINI
9114 Strada Place, Naples: 239-591-2583
www.bluemartinilounge.com/
The bartender here told me they feature "42 superior martinis," but I'm not quite sure what they mean by superior. (Expensive might be a better word.) I'm not big on the "specialty" cocktail craze that seems to have taken over the nation's nightlife hot spots. (Pomegranate juice in your drink?), but that's just me. A fun and lively atmosphere here.

Dancing nightly. Tapas menu.

DUSK
RITZ-CARLTON NAPLES
280 Vanderbilt Beach Rd, Naples, 239-598-6644
www.ritzcarlton.com
A nice elegant lounge on the first floor of the Ritz is a nice place to relax with fancy cocktails and really good sushi selections.

HAROLD'S PLACE
2555 Tamiami Trail N., Naples: 239-263-7254
www.naplesharoldsplace.com/
This little tiki bar (with mighty good burgers, I might add, as well as the grouper sandwich) is tucked behind the Quality Inn overlooking a pool, but it's a nice place to chill when the weather's good. As low key as it gets.

OLD NAPLES PUB

www.naplespubs.com
255 13th Ave S, Naples, 239-649-8200
Village on Venetian Bay, 4360 Gulf Shore Blvd., Naples, 239-262-2707
Soups, salads, sandwiches and entrees served for lunch and dinner in this cozy family-style pub in the heart of the fancy shopping to be enjoyed in the Third Street District. Gather around the century-old piano for a sing-along. The other location is in the Village on Venetian Bay in the Parkshore neighborhood where you'll find waterfront dining with a panoramic view.

SUNSET BEACH BAR
Naples Beach Hotel & Golf Club
851 Gulf Shore Blvd. N., Naples: 239-261-2222
www.naplesbeachhotel.com
Recently awarded the title of Naples' "Best Beach Bar" by Travel Channel, live entertainment every night.

SPAS

THE RITZ CARLTON
280 Vanderbilt Beach Rd., Naples: 239-514-6100
www.ritzcarlton.com
The three-floor Spa here was voted Best in Florida by readers of "Spa" magazine. It's no wonder why. They offer a complete range of services for body, mind and spirit.
Wraps and glows, global therapies, nail services, salon, wellness and personal training, wedding packages, aroma-reflex, facials, massage, you name

it. The web site is quite detailed and has a FAQ page that will answer a lot of your questions if you've never been to a first class spa before. **NOTE**: Spa services and facilities are only available to registered Ritz-Carlton, Naples beach and golf resort guests and Spa members. Local residents and non-resort guests can use the salon and facial services in **The Salon,** located on the Lobby Level of the Spa. This little requirement sort of forces you to stay here at the Ritz, but a good way around it is to book one night here, enjoy the spa, and then move off to another property where you might rather be.

INDEX

A

Arthur L. Allen Tennis Center, 55

B

BEACH HOUSE OF NAPLES, 39
BEACHES, 47
BELLASERA RESORT LUXURY HOTEL, 13
BIG MOMMA'S BICYCLES, 10
BLUE MARTINI, 71
BUSCH GARDENS, 57

C

C. ORRICO, 40
CAPRI FISH HOUSE RESTAURANT, 22
CITY SEAFOOD, 23
CORKSCREW SWAMP SANCTUARY, 48

D

DOCK AT CRAYTON COVE, 23
DOLPHIN EXPLORER, 48
DUSK, 72

F

Fifth Avenue South, 39
FINDICTIVE CHARTERS, 49

G

Greater Naples Marco Everglades Convention & Visitors Bureau, 7

H

H.B.'S ON THE GULF, 24
HAROLD'S PLACE, 72
HAWTHORN SUITES NAPLES, 14
HILTON MARCO ISLAND BEACH RESORT, 14
Hyatt House Naples, 25
HYATT HOUSE NAPLES/5TH AVENUE, 15

I

INN ON FIFTH, 15

J

JOE'S DINER, 25

L

LA PLAYA, 16
LATITUDE 26, 25
LEMON TREE INN, 16
LOCAL, 26
LOUIS VUITTON, 41
LOVING FINE JEWELRY, 41

M

M WATERFRONT GRILLE, 27
MANGO'S DOCKSIDE BISTRO, 27
MARCO BEACH OCEAN RESORT, 17
MARCO ISLAND, 7
MARCO ISLAND HISTORICAL MUSEUM, 50
MARCO ISLAND MARRIOTT RESORT & SPA, 17
MARISSA COLLECTIONS, 41
MEL'S DINER, 28
MIROMAR OUTLETS, 42

N

Naples Beach Hotel, 24
Naples Beach Hotel & Golf Club, 73
NAPLES BEACH HOTEL & GOLF CLUB, 18
NAPLES BOTANICAL GARDEN, 50
NAPLES DEPOT MUSEUM, 51
NAPLES MUSEUM OF ART, 52
Naples Train Museum, 51
NAPLES ZOO AT CARIBBEAN GARDENS, 53

O

OLD NAPLES PUB, 73
OLD NAPLES SURF SHOP, 43
OLDE MARCO ISLAND INN & SUITES, 19
OTTER MOUND PRESERVE, 53

P

PEACE, LOVE & LITTLE DONUTS, 43

R

RITZ CARLTON, 19, 76
RITZ-CARLTON NAPLES, 72
RIVERWALK AT TIN CITY, 28

S

SALE E PEPE, 29
SEA SALT, 30
Seafood, 22, 26, 34
SHULA'S STEAK HOUSE, 31
SMALLWOOD STORE, 53
SNOOK INN, 31
STAN'S IDLE HOUR, 32
SUNDAY BASH, 54
SUNSET BEACH BAR, 73
SUNSET GRILLE, 33

T

TENNIS, 55
Third Street South, 39
TIGERTAIL BEACH, 55
Tigertail Gift Shop, 54
TIN CITY, 56
TOMMY BAHAMA, 44
TRIAD SEAFOOD, 34
TRULUCK'S SEAFOOD, STEAK, AND CRAB HOUSE, 35

V

VERDI'S AMERICAN BISTRO, 36

W

WATERSIDE SHOPS, 45
WILLIAM PHELPS CUSTOM JEWELER, 44

Other Books by the Same Author

Andrew Delaplaine has written in widely varied fields: screenplays, novels (adult and juvenile), travel writing, journalism. His books are available in quality bookstores, libraries, as well as all online retailers.

JACK HOUSTON ST. CLAIR POLITICAL THRILLERS

On Election night, as China and Russia mass soldiers on their common border in preparation for war, there's a tie in the Electoral College that forces the decision for President into the House of Representatives as mandated by the Constitution. The incumbent Republican President, working through his Aide for Congressional Liaison, uses the Keystone File, which contains dirt on every member of Congress, to blackmail members into supporting the Republican candidate. The action runs from Election Night in November to Inauguration Day on January 20. Jack Houston St. Clair runs a small detective agency in Miami. His father is Florida Governor Sam Houston St. Clair, the Republican candidate. While he tries to help his dad win the election, Jack also gets hired to follow up on some suspicious wire transfers involving drug smugglers, leading him to a sunken narco-sub off Key West that has $65 million in cash in its hull.

AFTER THE OATH: DAY ONE
AFTER THE OATH: MARCH WINDS
WEDDING AT THE WHITE HOUSE

Only three months have passed since Sam Houston St. Clair was sworn in as the new President, but a lot has happened. Returning from Vienna where he met with

Russian and Chinese diplomats, Sam is making his way back to Flagler Hall in Miami, his first trip home since being inaugurated. Son Jack is in the midst of turmoil of his own back in Miami, dealing with various dramas, not the least of which is his increasing alienation from Babylon Fuentes and his growing attraction to the seductive Lupe Rodriguez. Fernando Pozo addresses new problems as he struggles to expand Cuba's secret operations in the U.S., made even more difficult as U.S.-Cuban relations thaw. As his father returns home, Jack knows Sam will find as much trouble at home as he did in Vienna.

WANT 3 **FREE** NOVELS?

If you like these writers--
Vince Flynn, Brad Thor, Tom Clancy, James Patterson, David Baldacci, John Grisham, Brad Meltzer, Daniel Silva, Don DeLillo

If you like these TV series –
House of Cards, Scandal, West Wing, The Good Wife, Madam Secretary, Designated Survivor

You'll love the **unputdownable** series about Jack Houston St. Clair, with political intrigue, romance, suspense.

Besides writing travel books, I've written political thrillers for many years. I want you to read my work!
Send me an email and I'll send you a link where you can download the 3 books, absolutely FREE.

Mention **this book** when you email me.

andrewdelaplaine@mac.com

www.ingramcontent.com/pod-product-compliance
Lightning Source LLC
Chambersburg PA
CBHW061502040426
42450CB00008B/1457